FOR ME AND MY FAMILY

Joyce Landorf

VISION HOUSE PUBLISHERS
Santa Ana, California 92705

Revised Standard Version Bible used by permission.

Verses marked TLB are taken from The Living Bible, Copyright 1971 by Tyndale House Publishers, Wheaton, Illinois. Used by permission.

For Me and My Family

CONTENTS

Chapter 1

NO TROUBLED FAMILIES

Did you know that there is no such thing as a troubled family? To hear some people talk today, you would think troubled families simply do not exist, but everywhere I look I find them. Yet the myth persists.

I saw the full impact of that "no troubled family" myth in a moderate-sized town on the southern edge of our eastern seacoast.

Family Forum, a weekend seminar taught by Dr. James Dobson and myself, was scheduled for this town.

During the two nights and one day of speaking, both Dr. Dobson and I would be covering such subjects as marriage, communication, raising families, self-worth, handling bereavement, and many practical ways of coping with some of the everyday stresses of living.

When I arrived from California, the chairperson was worried about the poor preregistration turnout.

"It's still early," I said, trying to calm her fears, but she would not be soothed.

"It's just that you don't know, Joyce, what I've gone through to get the Family Forum to this town, and you wouldn't believe the opposition I've had to battle!"

"Opposition from whom?" I asked.

"A minister in the big church down the street."

"How did he do it?"

"He said that Family Forum was coming to our town, and that it was strictly for 'troubled families.' He added that if the people *knew* any such families they might want to tell them about the Forum."

"Let me guess," I said, "You gave a party for troubled families, and nobody came."

"Right!" she answered. "It was a long time before even one person signed up."

I looked at her and said, "Of *course* no one signed up, wanted to come or, more accurately, needed to come because there *are* no 'troubled families' in your town!"

"Right!" she answered, and rolled her eyes in a brief show of helplessness.

Not to acknowledge the presence of troubled families is a disease not only of this town but many, many towns and cities covering all strata of people.

"Not My Family!"

It seems we know, if only from listening to the six o'clock news, that there must be a few troubled families. However, it's a remote kind of knowledge and our concern and awareness end with the newscaster's sign-off. We go into a kind of glassy-eyed denial and say troubled families don't live on our street; and certainly our own family is not in trouble.

We are a generation of people who are fond of chuckling smugly as we say, "Oh, we have a few differences of opinion in our family, a few weird relatives and some problems with our kids, but nothing big—nothing we can't handle."

If we are ever to overcome this widespread type of denial, we will have to start admitting the existence of family conflicts—from minor complaints and disagreements to big, obvious crisis problems—even among Christian, church-going families.

In many homes it's almost as if we do not dare to admit we have had a failure or a problem. We must make it the most well-kept secret of the year, and often we end up keeping the knowledge even from ourselves.

I know several individuals, perhaps you know some too, who have never uttered any of the following sentences: "It was my fault." "Whoops, I sure blew that one." "I completely misjudged the child." "I pounced before I had the facts." "It was my responsibility and I failed."

At this point I am not talking about the person who is "above" apologizing—while that's related here, it's yet another bag—but I am talking of the person who cannot accept the blame or responsibility for something gone wrong. The denial is so deep within them they refuse to see the problem at all.

In face of such denial, it is no wonder then that there were no "troubled families" in all of that town. It is also no wonder that of all the places Family Forum traveled to that year, Dr. Dobson and I encountered more broken, troubled, hurting individuals and families there than in the two previous seminars put together. No troubled families? False!

The sad, overwhelming truth confronts us on every level of our lives, and in all the media. There is hardly a home anywhere that has escaped it. *The American family, including the Christian family, is in deep, devastating trouble.*

It is a truth that we had better face. It's happening, not just to some non-Christian family out there somewhere, someplace, but right within my house and for my family.

Far too long the church has implied that if a mother and father are Christians then they are guaranteed a happy, trouble-free home. In real life, however, conflict, trouble, stress and crisis develop all too commonly. While statistics *do* show that the divorce rate is lower among practicing Christian couples, divorce is taking its toll from Christians as well as non-Christians. Particularly sad is that Christian homes have their share of abusive parents, alcohol, drug addiction, homosexual sons and daughters, and rebellious-hearted members. Sin has raised its ugly head in the *best* of homes.

You may disagree with me, that's your prerogative, but the Bible clearly states that the decay of the family has been going on for longer than any of us have lived.

Even under the ancient leadership of Sparta, the family was under fire. In Sparta's military dictatorship, mothers and fathers lived in separate quarters while children were raised somewhere else completely under state supervision. The goal of Sparta's training was to teach unfailing loyalty to their leader and the state.

Even now in communist-controlled countries, children are living, working, learning, studying, and playing together in a separated non-family environment. I feel certain that the world will see in a few years what havoc has been wrought by this destructive trend of raising children without parents, home, and families. What hope is there for adults who, as children, were stamped out of some giant sheet of cookie dough?

As the Family, So Goes the Nation

Many authorities have traced the history of family life from the past and have come up with almost exactly the same horrifying conclusions: if marriage and the family unit are devalued, dissolved, or picked to shreds and destroyed—so goes the nation that perpetrated the crime.

We Americans, with no dictatorial decrees, are seeing our families breaking up; one marriage in every three ending in divorce; juvenile crime and suicides up and climbing; and yet we are not under communist or state-enforced programs. So why do we have troubled families?

My pastor, Ted Cole, said it best. "It is from the erosion of a thousand forces."

Therein lies the complexity of the problem. Most of us agree and know deep down in our viscera that our families are in crisis situations, or at least are troubled, but because of a "thousand forces" eating silently and darkly away at us from within, we are hard put to deal with it. Answers are hard to find. It's easier to deny it.

On Saturday in the eastern town that "had no troubled families" a handsome young man waited to talk to me after my session with the men on *Tough and Tender*.

It was hard for him to speak, but he pulled himself

together and, in a very soft but almost frantic voice, he said, "Mrs. Landorf, I have a gun in my car outside. On Thursday I was going to use it on myself, but my wife asked me to please come to this Family Forum. So we came in a last ditch effort to help our marriage. I didn't want to come, but I agreed anyway.

"Neither my wife nor I are Christians. I don't love her anymore. I am having an affair with another woman, and all the lying and cheating I've been doing has finally caught up with me. Up until this weekend I thought suicide was the only answer. Now, I don't know."

Briefly, for I had to speak in the next session, we stood in the hall talking. I spoke of his real need—the one of turning over his life and sins to the forgiving God of mercy.

After we prayed together, I thought: Are there troubled families in this town or mine? Yes! Is there any hope, any joy, or peace for families? Yes! Yes! Yes!

But we must first admit there are tremendous needs; and second, we must begin to take a realistic inventory of our lives.

The welfare of the Christian family and home is in jeopardy unless we make it "Number One" on our list of important priorities.

Chapter 2

"IT'S NOT MY TURN TO TAKE OUT THE TRASH."

When you were little, did you and your brothers or sisters take turns doing certain duties, or were you assigned one or two specific chores?

Our life with our two children was a bit of a mix between those two principles, but I can remember an occasional exasperated child when he or she said, "It's not *my* turn to take out the trash!"

Taking on a responsibility of any magnitude, large or small, has always pained us to some degree. Assuming the immense load of responsibility involving the keeping of a family together has given more than one mother or father years of Excedrin headaches.

Who is really responsible for the keeping together of the Christian home? Is it the sole work of the husband, wife, church, or school? Is it the relegating of various duties and chores to certain people? Or is it a combination of things?

God seems to have clearly wanted the family to be headed by the husband, but fully supported in attitude and deed by the wife.

The first mention of marriage in the Old Testament says—"Therefore a man leaves his father and his mother and cleaves to his wife, and they become one flesh" (Gen. 2:24, RSV).

The picture I get here is of a strong man, definitely the head of his newly-started home. But he is not expected to do it alone. Rather, he *and* his wife stand together, cleaving to each other in the marriage commitment.

I firmly believe that when two people commit themselves to God and cleave to each other they can become so unified in choosing purposeful goals, so unanimous in determining which priorities are important, and so wise in learning what direction God is leading, that shared responsibility is a lot less painful and is far more easily accomplished than responsibility borne alone.

But over and over again I am confronted by real people who are tired—no, exhausted—by the lonely load of total responsibility.

There's the woman who has to do all the disciplining of the children because her husband had an overly stern father who beat him for any infraction of the rules. So now, as an adult, he reneges on any disciplining. His wife is always the "bad guy," and the kids know Dad will let them get away with anything.

Then there's the man who believes that working nine to twelve hours a day, bringing home a pay check, providing food and housing for his wife and children are the total sum of his responsibility. So neither his wife nor his children ever get to know him, nor do they find any level of communication between themselves.

There's also the man who is a secret Christian. He rarely talks or lives Christianity, and very little spiritual fruit is produced in his life. He assumes no spiritual responsibility at all for his home or family.

I suppose what concerns me the most, as I talk with hundreds of people each month, is not only the lack of two people sharing their God-given responsibilities, but the number of times I am confronted by the husband's failure to take any of the spiritual leadership.

By far the most common complaint from Christian women is that their Christian husband will not be the spiritual leader or even minutely help in that direction.

I'm personally glad that Paul qualifies his statements about the husband and wife relationship, particularly in the areas of responsible leadership. As a wife I'm to submit myself to my husband *as* I submit myself to the Lord. (See Ephesians 5.)

How is anyone able to submit to the Lord? Practicing, spirit-filled Christians know it's all done with *attitudes*.

Paul says virtually the same thing for husbands when he says that men are to love their wives *as* Christ loved the Church. What woman, in her right mind, can refuse to submit to a man who loves her as Christ loved the Church? What man can resist a woman who loves him in the exact way she lovingly submits to the Lord? Not many, that's for sure.

Nowhere in any of Ephesians 5 do I see either the husband or the wife assuming complete responsibility for the growth or development of the Christian home.

Marriage was not meant to be a one-man or a one-woman show. It was meant to be a team effort: Two people committed to the same goals, living and existing in a Christ-centered, working marriage.

So here it is, one of the "thousand forces" which are tearing Christian families apart: the failure of the husband, the wife, or both, to accept their God-appointed responsibilities for the family and home.

Ask yourself some of these questions about your family: 1. Is the man the *loving* leader? 2. Is the man an absentee husband and father? 3. Is the woman a true helpmate and partner? 4. Is the woman the domineering pacesetter? 5. Is one or the other unwilling or unable to talk about conflicts? 6. Do both parents agree on and enforce loving discipline with their children?

We need to clearly and honestly audit ourselves to evaluate how we stand in a God-arranged marriage and whose turn it is to do what.

Chapter 3

JOSHUA'S COMMITMENT

The life and words of Joshua continually challenge my heart each time I read the Word of God. Near the end of his life, Joshua tells the leaders of Israel, the elders, judges, and officers, "I am an old man now" (Josh. 23:2, TLB). He then traces all that God's hand has done for them during his long life as their leader. He instructs Israel to follow God's laws and "to keep on loving him" (v. 11). He tells Israel that serving God should be the highest priority of all life. Then he asks them to choose, that very day, whom they would serve. His key statement comes when he says, "But as for me and my family, we will serve the Lord" (Josh. 24:15 TLB).

He didn't say, "I, Joshua, will serve the Lord." He defines and strengthens the statement, takes upon his shoulders the responsibility where it has been laid, and says, "As for me and my family, we will serve the Lord." He told the whole nation that day, once and for all, of his tough, unyielding decision to obey and serve God with his life and the lives of his entire household for whatever time he had left. He never implied that Mrs. Joshua would handle all the spiritual chores. He took the reins in his own hands and clearly knew the road he'd take.

Somehow Christian men have forgotten Joshua's fine example and have abdicated leadership in the home. It was as if developing prayer and family devotions, getting off to Sunday School, building a love of God through consistent godly, daily living was as much woman's work and calling as having babies and cooking the evening meal. Men simply withdrew when it was time to pray or to counsel their children spiritually.

A wife may be absolutely starving to death spiritually because a husband is not willing to be the tough, consistent high priest of his home and family unit. A man shrugs his shoulders and says, "Well, all that's woman's work," or "I don't know how to pray," or (and this is classic) "I'm a man of few words and all that religious stuff is personal anyway." And so he slips off into the welcome oblivion of his work, schooling, or hobby as easily as butter slides off a hot knife. Vaguely he hopes that if he merely attends church, joins the choir, or becomes an usher, he will appease his wife (and God) and give his children the Christian training they should have.

Most of the time it doesn't work out too well. For instance, just about the time his children hit the tornado-like times of their teenage years, they begin getting into one mess after another. He feels he can't cope or understand their behavior because, "After all, I've raised them to be good Christians." By that, he really means he has gotten up on Sundays to go to church because of his wife's insistence. Since he's never been the spiritual pacesetter in his home, and real Christianity is being lived and practiced reluctantly for one hour on Sundays, why should he be surprised when his children's faith in God collapses?

God Is Here to Help

Men, if you feel spiritual responsibility is absolutely above and beyond your abilities, let me quickly assure you: *God, the One who sees all hearts and understands all limitations, honors His Word—and your intentions.* You don't have to accept this responsibility alone.

One guarantee came when Paul and Silas were talking to their jailor and fellow prisoners. They were asked by the jailor, "What must I do to be saved?" The two giants of the faith answered, "Believe in the Lord Jesus Christ and the Lord will save you and your entire household" (see Acts 16:30-32). That verse was written to you, to all men and for all mankind; God wasn't kidding around. As I just said, He is a God who will honor His Word and your intentions.

I have often wondered just how fast I would have come along in my spiritual life had my husband, Dick, been unwilling to take spiritual leadership as he saw God's leading. I have an idea that without Dick's efforts, his pacesetting in spiritual things and his constant seeking of God's will and direction, I might not have had the strength, willpower, or courage to continue as a Christian woman. I'm fully aware that my attitudes contribute to the healthy or unhealthy mental state of my entire household, but it is the husband's responsibility to give spiritual and emotional security to his family unit. Many a woman, stronger than I, has given up in her obedience to God because of the weary, constant struggle with a husband who would not, could not, or did not allow God to develop his spiritual assignments.

If you, as a Christian husband, are a secret Christian—one who down in the depths of your heart has asked God to forgive—but you have never told anyone on earth of the decision, and your wife and children only suspect your status, there is marvelous news for you. You can come out of hiding and take your stand!

First of all, you've come into a fortune. Romans 8:17 says that Christians are heirs of God, and joint-heirs with Christ . . ." So there you have it: you have won the lottery ticket to end all lottery tickets! Never lose sight of that thought. There is a slight catch, however. We are very clearly told by Jesus Himself in Matthew 10:32, 33 (RSV), "So everyone who acknowledges me before men, I also will acknowledge before my Father who is in heaven; but whoever denies me before men, I also will deny before my Father who is in heaven." So it seems to me the beginning point of being a spiritual leader starts the second you publicly state your intention and position as a Christian man—*before others*.

"Oh," but a man says, "I don't have to tell my wife or anyone else I'm a Christian. I can just decide inside." In light of Jesus' own words, I'm sure the decision to be quiet about one's faith is a *decision for denial*. It would be sad for a man to stand before God at the end of his lifetime and hear the heart-chilling words of God, "Depart from Me—I've never known you."

The Bible does not tell you, as a husband, that after you become a Christian you should go out, set up roadblocks in your neighborhood, stop each car, bus, or tricycle, and tell people you are a Christian; but it says simply to *acknowledge* whom you have chosen to serve in some way—to some other human being. Start with your wife!

I'll never forget Dick's statement of choice when he came home, took me by the shoulders so many years ago, and solemnly, sternly and without hesitation, stated, "Joyce, I don't care what you think or say, but today I made up my mind. I am going to be a Christian. I mean a real honest-to-God Christian—a Christian husband and father."

Thus Dick chose his pulpit—our home—and began his ministry as our high priest. It was also trial and error all the way! Dick didn't know how to be the spiritual leader any more than any husband may know right now. All he *did know* was that God intended for him to do it; so, blindly, he began. He brought God's spiritual security into our lives and it never went smoothly. However, his determination paid off.

I suppose it's the word *determination* which most characterizes Joshua. He stubbornly willed himself into the spiritual leadership of his home. I don't think it was any easier then for Joshua than it is now for my husband Dick or any other man.

A study made by the University of Southern California on parents' religious influence found that church-going habits of youths (aged 16-26) *and* how they rated themselves in religious devotion were most similar to the *father's* habits and responses whether high or low.

The study also showed that when both parents

went to church regularly, or both never attended, the corresponding behavior was usually the case with their children.

I found this study to be unusual in that the data gathered contradicted the widespread idea that mothers are solely responsible for their children's religious beliefs and training. It laid the spiritual responsibility on the husband, exactly as the Bible has done all along.

So in the long run, it is the father who determines whom his family will serve and love, just as Joshua said so long ago—

But as for me and my family,
we will serve the Lord.

Joshua 24:15

Chapter 4

PRACTICAL PAYING AND PRAYING

The statistics can never be fully tabulated, but it's been established by psychologists and marriage counselors that 75 percent of the couples in our country today live in a state of emotional divorce. They live together, yet are worlds apart.

Because so many of these are "good Christian" marriages, I am convinced that they live not only in the state of an emotional divorce but with a spiritual one as well.

I speak with authority here as I spent five hellish, nightmarish years drowning in an emotional and spiritual divorce in my own marriage until Christ became our deliverer.

One of the first things we learned in putting an end to our spiritual divorce involved acknowledging that we needed each other and other Christians. There is a small but powerful verse in Hebrews which tells us not to forsake "the assembling of ourselves together"

(Heb. 10:25, KJV). The author was not trying to up church attendance so he could win some contest. He was really giving us a way to stay healthy as children of God.

My husband's first decision, spiritually, was to find us a church where we could not only worship the Lord and give our children specific Christian training, but fellowship with other believers.

My husband's decision began a fantastic ministry in our lives through that church, its pastor, its music, and its host of *real friends*. His decision made possible a substantial part of our children's religious training and provided the Christian security they so desperately needed in today's world of shifting mores.

We need to experience a time of worship to God in His house, to give Him tithes and gifts, and to hear the singing of the choir and congregation. We need to be warmed by a friend who whispers, "All week I've been thinking about you and have been holding you up in prayer before our Lord." We need the message that streams forth out of the heart of our pastor, and we *need* the presence of *each other*.

My husband had become the spiritual pacesetter of our house in choosing a church home for us, but it began to be more involved than that. Choosing a church was just the very first step in being the people God wanted us to become.

Tackling the Tithe

I suppose tithing our income was the toughest spiritual decision Dick was ever to make. I mean—touch a man's wallet, particularly a banker's, and you've put your fingers on his heart and pulsebeat.

Financially, there is no *right* time to begin to tithe. You are never at a place where you will not *feel* tithing.

At first Dick gave to the church after all bills were paid. Usually it was not a tenth of our income, but just a small scrap or token. However, he began to feel a little guilty about "holding out on God" in the light of how extremely well our personal lives were going. Our marriage, since we had really accepted Christ, made a fantastic turnabout.

We were surprisingly happy in spite of eating beans and hamburgers and not having one extra dime left over each month. We knew it had to be God working the changes; it seemed only right that we give Him at least what the Bible said should amount to a tenth of our income.

At first nothing happened, but Dick began writing out the tithe check *first* after payday. Then he wrote the bills and did the bookkeeping. Neither of us remembers when the joy hit, because it was such a subtle thing. But somewhere in those early, rather sparse years of giving, tithing phased from duty to a quiet gladness. Our income was very low, so tithing was painful; yet strange as it seemed, we always had a place to live, and we never ran out of money or food at the end of the month. True, there was absolutely nothing left over for years and years. After paying our tithe to God off the top and not the bottom (even when we had hospital—emergency bills) we saw all needs met.

One of God's most fantastic promises says, "For if you give, you will get! Your gift will return to you in full and overflowing measure, pressed down, shaken together to make room for more, and running over. Whatever measure you use to give—large or small—

will be used to measure what is given back to you" (Luke 6:38, TLB).

In Malachi 3:7-12, the prophet is telling the people how they have robbed God and what would happen to them if they really tithed. "Bring all the tithes into the storehouse so that there will be food enough in my Temple; if you do, I will open up the windows of heaven for you and pour out a blessing so great you won't have room enough to take it in!" (v. 10, TLB). We serve a God who is still faithful to His promises. This same God is a master financier. He very plainly says to invest in Him and He will see to your increases. Your stock will go up and your financial rewards will astound you.

We realized, during our early years of Christian life, that God did not need our money, even though He asked for it; but rather we needed the great experience of giving and sharing with God. Once we began tithing we found that God blessed our lives in three ways: We had financial wisdom—to our surprise; we had paying investments; and we had an open opportunity account which taught us to use what we had, not what we wished we had.

Daily Bible reading—both individually and with the family—began, too.

My husband's Bible reading is confined to our dinnertime readings, but his prayer life knows no such limits. He has accepted another ministry—that of being a praying man. Like tithing, it never came easy; always, even to this day, praying means shutting off or putting down something else to make time for it. Tough job? You bet!

Since Dick is a man of few words, he found that in his personal prayer life he was better equipped to remember the needs in our lives if he had a record of written requests. So, early in the development of our Christian lives, we began to see the incredible influence our little spiral notebooks had on us, our friends, and our children. Our son, Rick, is married and lives in a nearby town; our daughter, Laurie, is 22 and living in a college dorm; but both kids still peek and check our lists to see if they are on it and to take our spiritual temperature, as it were.

While Dick's personal prayer life has seen many God-answered miracles, I suspect our prayer life together as partners has been the most rewarding. It has given us unexpected dividends and benefits we never, never considered when we first began praying together. Now, I wish I could tell you that right from the second we became Christians we had a marvelous prayer life that was completely satisfying in every way. But that's not how it really happened.

We were novices at praying *separately*, much less *together*. Fumbling and embarrassed as he was, Dick found out-loud praying essentially painful. My noisy nature allowed me a bit more freedom in out-loud praying, but it was remarkable how easily Dick went to sleep while I prayed. (Of course, we had the added hazard of having our prayer time together just after we went to bed, but it was the only time we could make for prayer.) While Dick prayed I found I could mentally redecorate the bathroom or let my mind wander to any number of projects. It's no wonder we soon lost interest in this boring concept of prayer.

A New Way to Pray

We might have missed forever the most enriching time of our lives had it not been for a flight to San

Francisco I took with Dr. Ralph Byron. He is a famed surgeon at City of Hope Hospital in Duarte, California, and a man who is equally adept at performing surgery in an operating room and at teaching the lesson on Sunday to his class in church. Dr. Byron was the speaker that night for a banquet in San Francisco and I was to provide the special music for the program. He is a very busy man, yet I just knew he prayed with his wife! I was sure of it, so I blurted out, "Dr. Byron, just *when* do you and Dorothy pray?"

He smiled and answered, "Just before we go to sleep at night."

"But," I questioned, "doesn't one of you go to sleep before the other finishes?"

He looked directly at me, and got to the heart of my probing with—"Ah, I see you and Dick are not praying the right way."

And then Dr. Ralph Byron gave me one of life's most valuable lessons on prayer. The things he taught me that night have turned our prayer into one of the most beautiful times of our lives.

"Dick," I shook him out of a deep sleep. "Honey, I've got to tell you what Dr. Byron told me about prayer tonight." He couldn't wake up completely, but he was aware it was 2:00 A. M. and I was home safely from the airport.

I pestered him into a wakeful but blurry-eyed awareness and he said, "Okay, give me the plan and we'll take ten minutes' time to pray, and then I'm going back to sleep."

Forty-five minutes later he said, in a surprised way, "Why did you stop so soon?"

Dr. Byron had suggested that we take turns each night at being the leader or introducer of requests.

This night it was my turn and in one short sentence I introduced and prayed conversationally for subject number one. Then Dick prayed a short sentence for subject one. Next I introduced and prayed on subject two and Dick followed. We repeated the process until we had covered about seven items. It had been so interesting, so like talking with God in a three-way conversation, we had both completely lost track of time. Our ten-minute limit had jumped into forty-five flying minutes!

The next night it was Dick's turn to introduce the requests of his heart. Within a week several strange things began happening. First of all, at dinner one night I said, "Well, how did it go at work today?"

Dick matter-of-factly answered, "Oh, just fine." But later that same night, when he introduced subject number four, he prayed, "Lord, help me to know how to handle George and the serious problems he's creating at the bank."

My first thought was, "For Pete's sake—George who?" Then I realized what Dick could not share at the dinner table (or in any conversation with me) he felt perfectly free to present by prayer to the Lord. I remember praying intensely for old George what's-his-name that night and being just thrilled that Dick had shared a real need in his life. (Even if it was in a sneaky, roundabout way!)

Next we began to notice that on my night to give my requests I would pray for Dick's requests. On Dick's nights, many of my concerns would show up on his lists. The bond of love grows deep when we see our partner caring, remembering, and praying for our need and our request. I'll never get over the first time, on my husband's night to introduce requests, he ended his prayer time by praying, "Lord, thank You for my dear wife. I love her so much. Give her a good night's sleep and great day tomorrow. Amen."

If, after so many years of marriage, you can fall in love all over again with the same person, that was the moment for me. How strange it was—there we were praying together because we knew we should (almost like a duty); but suddenly we found ourselves, because of prayer, falling deeply in love with each other. I remember quiet tears streaming down my face in the darkness that night. I had heard my husband tell God how grateful he was for me and that he loved me. It was the most romantic thing he'd ever done.

If I could wave a magic wand for husbands in regard to their prayer life, I would wish several very important things:

1. *Make the time for conversational prayer with your wife.* It does not always need to be the same amount of time—your needs differ from day to day—but take whatever time you need. It's important to keep our vertical channels open to God as well as our horizontal communication channels open to each other.

2. *Keep your requests simple, honest, and liberally sprinkled with genuine thankfulness.*

3. *Listen to your wife's requests with all your hearing ability.* She may be giving you many clues as to her emotional and spiritual temperature. You may hear much more than verbal intonations and this may be one of the very best ways God has in mind for you to understand her inner tickings.

4. *Ask God to give you a keen sensitivity to know when to drop everything and right-then-and-there pray aloud.* I mean this for your wife's and your children's prayer life as well.

Once I was stranded in Georgia. I phoned collect to my husband. All I said was, "Dick, I've just been dumped off after my speaking engagement, I don't have flight reservations, it's raining and. . . ."

He broke into my running disaster report and said, "Dear Jesus, my wife is 3,000 miles away. I do not understand the mix-ups and why she is left alone, but I ask You now to calm her. Lord, take care of her right now, give her that quiet peace that only You can give and do for her what I cannot do today. Bring her quietly and safely home to us. Thank You, Lord, right now for what You are doing. Amen."

Even before he finished my hysteria left; then we calmly discussed flight plans, what to do about my hotel bill, etc., and all was worked out. It didn't stop raining, but my husband had prayed *instantly and out loud* for me, and my confidence in making plans was restored.

5. *Be real in praying*. Your wife needs to hear you pray, honestly from your heart. She needs to see you cry over the heartaches of people around you, and, most of all, she needs to feel your love of God. All this can be accomplished through your praying together.

6. *Before you pray, check out your attitude and treatment of your wife*. Peter suggested that if a man was having trouble praying and his prayers weren't too effective, he should examine how he was treating his wife. "You husbands must be careful of your wives, being thoughtful of their needs and honoring them as the weaker sex. Remember that you and your wife are partners in receiving God's blessings, and if you don't treat her as you should, your prayers will not get ready answers" (1 Peter 3:7, TLB). *Evidently*

the blessings in your life depend on your treatment of your wife as your partner.

Being the spiritual leader means being a spirit-filled man who commands in love, who teaches in love, and who respects others in love. Actually, again, it's the old Joshua-policy of choosing, this day, whom you will serve and saying, "As for me, and my family, we will serve the Lord."

Chapter 5

I'M LISTENING, BUT I CAN'T HEAR

Just this week I heard of a young couple who may be headed for divorce. Both are Christians and when they entered marriage less than two years ago, both thought their marriage was conceived in heaven and made to last. Now both are disillusioned and frustrated beyond belief.

It seems he won't talk to her. Whenever she says, "Can we talk about this?" he answers, "Why do we have to discuss negative things?" and without waiting for her answer he immediately leaves the room and shuts himself up in the bedroom. They are at a most impressive impasse.

Another woman I know recalled that their marriage was about to dissolve because she couldn't get her husband to talk with her. Then together they agreed to go to a communications seminar and one thought spoken by the minister changed their marriage's destiny. The husband was challenged to "*learn* how to talk to his wife or lose their marriage." Wisely he took the advice, and their life together began to blossom and grow into what God had foreseen.

Talking started out simply enough when we were about two years old. As we grew older we began to understand and comprehend terms more readily, and generally felt we could talk quite well by our teen years. Most of us entered adulthood with a small dose of smugness, confident that communicating with others was no big deal.

If you are like me, though, it was a sad and rude awakening to find the doors of communication firmly shut after a year of marriage. I found when loving, honest communication stopped, it sealed my husband and me off from each other. In retrospect, we found that the lack of talking and listening had preceded the death of our marriage by years.

Often I am involved in marital counseling. Sometimes after a couple has shared their trouble spots with me I ask them this question: "Can you pinpoint a time or event when one or both of you stopped feeling and caring for each other?" Their answer usually involves communication.

The wife says, "We used to talk for hours when we were dating, but he stopped talking to me once we were married."

The husband retorts, "I'd listen to her if she actually said anything, but I hate all that small talk."

The wife cracks back with, "That small talk you just described is about your home and your children. Don't you care about them?"

"Sure, I do," he continues, "but you're always yakking at me, and it's just easier to turn you off." You see, talking is only one-half of the popsicle; the other half is listening. Communication is a combination of both.

Since most of us see ourselves as pretty good talkers, I'd like to spend time on the listening part of communication. I pray this chapter will open some long-closed doors between husbands and wives.

In our family room I have framed 8" X 10" pictures of each member of our family. Dick's picture is my favorite. His chin is resting in his hands and he is looking away from the camera. Actually, we were talking at a table during a friend's wedding rehearsal dinner. I absolutely love it because I was the one Dick was so ardently listening to. I've seen that interested, loving look a hundred times, and it has been captured on film for me to cherish always. It's a portrait of loving communication, even if it is only the listening half.

The Lost Art of Listening

Listening is almost a lost art. It's as tough as making the decisions and being the spiritual leader of your house, men, but it can be done. Here are some areas to examine and probe involving a husband's listening attitudes and habits.

1. *Have you already stopped listening?* Some women begin talking at the moment of birth, and a steady stream follows each moment of their lives forever after, but others have developed a nonstop flow of talk for other reasons. Many times a compulsive talker is really shouting to be heard by someone. The more bored you look, the more you yawn, the more you watch the dog or TV, the harder she talks. She just talks all the more to compensate.

When was the last time you asked these questions of your wife? "How do you feel about . . .?" and/or "What happened here at home today?" Do you ever intersperse her remarks with, "You may be right, Hon"? If your wife feels you are not willing to listen to her, she has two options: to talk louder and harder; or to talk less and withdraw. Either way, it's very hard on the marriage.

Just last night my husband asked me how I felt physically during my recent speaking engagements in Seattle. When he asked the question, he looked directly at me (ignoring the dog) and quietly waited for me to answer. He gave me all the go-ahead signals to talk. I didn't feel threatened by someone else capturing his attention. His eyes were on me. I knew he was listening—not just to my words but to the real message I was trying to convey. I gave him the facts, but I sensed he was after more than facts. He was really after my *feelings*. I was free to sit back and explain those feelings in unhurried detail!

Whenever we *listen for feelings* instead of information, we are on the way to being real listeners. A wife longs for even a few minutes of a husband's time in real listening.

2. *Do you listen without presuming or judging?* The man who hates his wife's small talk is a man who presumes he knows everything she is going to say before she says it. There is a verse in Proverbs which says, "What a shame—yes, how stupid!—to decide before knowing the facts!" (18:13, TLB). Yet we are guilty of such stupidity.

As most of us listen to someone, we try to decide how we will answer them when they've finished. Surveys show we only hear about 20 percent of what is said; if that's true, and if our thoughts prejudge what's being said, we are in big trouble as listeners. It is easier to be talkers. It requires real toughness and self-discipline to be *hearing listeners*.

3. *Do you ever listen by touching?* Listening is not always done by the ears; sometimes it involves holding or touching.

Over and over, as our children were growing up, I hugged Rick or Laurie while they wept. Sometimes I knew the exact nature of their conflict, other times I had no idea. As their sobs subsided, I did not ask, "What's wrong—why the tears—what's happened?" It was enough to hold them, smooth their hair, and just *be there*. Just as many times as I recall my holding our children, I can remember Dick walking into our home and my running to his open arms. What a way to listen, to care, and to feel with someone.

After our infant son David died, I was recovering from a Caesarean section and went to my doctor's office for a postnatal examination. I had not seen my doctor since David died and I'll never forget our meeting. It was soon after surgery so Dick had brought me to the doctor's office in my nightie and robe. I was very weak and the nurses helped me up on the examining table. Then everyone left me alone to wait for the doctor. When he came in he said absolutely nothing. He did not give me a phony, cheery greeting. He merely walked over to me and very tenderly put both of his hands over mine. I looked up at him and with teary eyes he turned his head to the window and continued to hold my hands—but he never *spoke* a word. What he communicated in those brief seconds spoke volumes to my heart. It even brought a measure of healing, because I knew he deeply cared about my loss; yet nothing was said then or ever.

Sometimes when your wife is frustrated beyond belief over a rebellious teenager, a critical remark made by a relative, or maybe by an extra job—try touching. I'm suggesting you give the touching and holding technique a chance. It might really show her *you do hear her*, and *she may hear you* better than she's ever heard you before.

4. *Are you communicating in honesty*? We all talk and listen at different levels of honesty. It was John Powell who outlined for us the five levels of communication which most of us use daily. In his book, *Why Am I Afraid to Tell You Who I Am?* he listed these: Level 5—Cliche Conversation; Level 4—Reporting the Facts About Others; Level 3—My Ideas and Judgments; Level 2—My Feelings and Emotions; Level 1—Complete Emotional and Personal Truthful Communication.

Most of us are pretty good at Level 5 with its no-risk policy in effect. You can't get hurt by saying, "Hi, how are you?" But getting down to Level 1 requires real honesty. Sometimes if we are open and honest we are rejected by the other person, and often that's too big a risk to chance.

If we are to communicate in honesty, we are going to have to wait for the best time and then present our feelings. Timing is very important. We must not store all our little grudges in gunnysacks and hold them too long, for *held grudges* become too large to handle.

When we do talk about our grudges, conflicts, and stressful problems we need to handle them in non-abusive language.

That's the form of talking together where you say, "I know this may sound silly of me, but I need to talk to you about such and such." It is also the language of lovers.

Two people who have earned the respect of each other have the right to have a kind, loving, open honesty with one another. This vehicle makes it possible for them to work out the conflicts of their hearts. The key to nonabusive language, though, is making sure you discuss the problem. Do not attack the person, because all that does is destroy his feelings of self-worth. When he sees his self-image being destroyed, he becomes hostile and defensive. Then all you've got is a rip-roaring argument with both parties flailing away at each other in hot anger. Stick with the issue at hand (don't confuse this issue by digging up old issues, either) and leave out the personalities as much as possible.

5. *Do you communicate through written words?* Talking and listening are certainly forceful tools of communication, but sometimes the most meaningful tool is that of writing.

6. *Are you a gut-level listener?* We all come so close to missing what people are really saying around us. Sometimes it's too much work, too many pressures, too many fears or risks involved, and so we do not listen with our gut-level intuition. It is a precious gift to give to your marriage if you can listen to your partner with all your soul.

Time to Listen

7. *Do you take time to listen?* In a study by Cornell University, 200 fathers were asked to estimate how much time they spent daily with each of their children. The men estimated they spent an average of fifteen minutes per day per child. Then the children were fitted with tape-recording devices, and the actual time was clocked. The final studies showed that

the average time each man actually spent with a child per day was thirty-seven seconds!

If there were a way to conduct the same study on husbands and wives, I wonder what the length of time would be? Each couple needs to find the *sharing time* of the day. Ours happens to include a couple of times, but the first one is just after Dick gets home. Our children are grown now and they are not climbing all over him for his attention, so the first twenty minutes are mine.

Generally I stand around waiting. I lose five minutes of dialogue this way, but men need a buffer zone of time during which they shed their working responsibilities. It's difficult for them to tune in to home life with any degree of eagerness when their job is still on their backs like a heavy load of bricks. (I think I understand why so many men stop off at a local bar for a beer or two before going home. It's their buffer zone between work and home, where they're expected to listen to more problems and conflicts from the family.)

Eventually he asks, "Well, what happened today that I should know about?"

A word to wives at this point. Don't tell him anything but good news. The bills and broken-appliance news can wait until after he's had supper. Most men tend to be grumpy before they eat, so save the bad biggies for later.

Another time we have for talking and listening is after the dinner hour. However, because of schedules this is not on a regular basis. That's probably why the time just after Dick gets home is so important to keeping our lives open to each other. One other time which is very special to us is Saturday morning at breakfast. We take longer at this meal than any other because *we talk*. Men, when do you and your wife have a quick ten-minute dialogue about the day's events? It really doesn't matter when you have it, but that you do have it.

Second, is there any time in your week when you and your wife can have a lunch, breakfast, or "whatever" together without the kids, friends, or relatives? A well-known minister and his wife take one day a month to go off together. They have four children, but one day a month just the husband and the wife go away together. That day (only twelve days each year) has held their marriage solidly together for years, in spite of their crushing and hectic schedules.

At this point you may be saying, "Joyce, first of all I don't have time at home to talk because I work eighteen hours a day. Besides we don't have any way to spend a day away from home like the minister you know." I do understand about long hours and the unavailability of time to talk, but you may have to decide which priority is more important: making the money to support the family, or keeping a family together emotionally. The old question from Matthew: " . . . what is a man profited if he shall gain the whole world, and lose his own soul?" (16:26, KJV), is properly brought into focus here. You may have to seriously reconsider which is truly more important to you.

All of us are going to see our youngsters grow up and leave us to begin homes of their own. When that day comes, what will it be like in your house? Will you sit across from your wife, drink your morning coffee, and read your paper without noticing or acknowledging her? Do you remember the coffee commercial that showed a husband and wife at breakfast? He read the paper and she read a book. He tasted his coffee and liked it, so he put down his paper and said, "It's really good." She lowered her book. He took a good look at her and said, "When did you get your nose fixed?" She gave him a funny stare and answered, "Two years ago. When did you grow bald?" He replied, "Eight years ago!" I always had a funny-sad reaction when I really listened to that commercial. They were living together, sharing the same table, bed, and house; yet they never saw or spoke to one another.

It is up to you—in your house—to set the wheels of listening in motion.

Chapter 6

CROWNING YOUR EFFORTS WITH SUCCESS

As a wife and mother I am acutely aware of how my attitudes, my moods, or my spirit influences the success of the family's relationships.

It's true, we women can often determine the way a family grows close or fades away. But if my husband does not fully support me in verbal and nonverbal attitudes, if he criticizes my job, or worse, never gives any approval to my efforts, I'm sunk!

In order to bring healing and joy to our troubled families it will take both of us, working hard and working *daily* to achieve it.

I do not want to be a single parent, a widowed woman, or a one-woman-show—I want desperately to be a team member with the man I love.

There are two words which come to my mind as I write this chapter on success in our family lives. One is *allowances*, and the other is *accepting*. Both these words are directed towards self and others.

Let me write out Ephesians 4:2, (TLB) my way, for clearer understanding, Paul says, "1. Be humble and gentle. 2. Be patient with each other 3. Make allowance for each other's faults, (Why? How?) because of your love."

Another translation says, "Forbearing one another in love" (KJV).

Too often a man and a woman are not at all willing to make an allowance for someone's idiosyncrasies, habits, or quirks. They end up spending a whole lifetime chiding, criticizing, even teasing the person for their faults. Biblically they are on dangerous ground, for clearly we are told to overlook faults and bear each other up.

I agree with the psychologists who believe that the majority of the time a man gets his feelings of self-worth from his job, employer, or the men around him. A woman, if she is not employed, must get her feelings of self-esteem from her husband. If he fails her in this, the chances are she will begin to search for it, either from her children or from someone outside the home.

The Christian husband and wife have a responsibility to encourage, make allowances, and verbally support each other. But over and over again, in my conversations with people, I find that the husband, preoccupied with work or set in his ways, refuses to make any "allowances" for his wife or children. Or, the wife has given, given, given for years and is simply not capable of "giving" any more.

Just this week I received a letter from a lovely young wife and mother. It was a "follow-up" kind of note, and I want to share it with you.

Several years ago I met Kay and Ted in a workshop session where I was talking about family life.

Ted was a "knife-licker" at the table, and having manners, making allowances, or encouraging his wife with acts and words were just not his bag.

They left that seminar and God really did a number (as my kids would say) on dear Ted. Ted was convinced about some of his manners and attitudes and he began immediately to change.

Kay's letter said it all so beautifully:

"Dear Joyce,

I've thought of you so often this past year and have seen your influence in our lives so much that I just wanted to share a little with you.

Since it's been some time since we've seen you, let me introduce myself. I'm the knife-licker's wife. Remember?

How our lives have changed!

A year ago we moved to Colorado and have been in the process of being 'molded' by our Heavenly Father.

Joyce, we've had the most difficult year of our lives—if you look at it through the world's eyes—and the most beautiful, if seen from the loving eyes of Jesus.

It has been a year of great uncertainty, many adjustments, and a devastating financial setback. But through it all has been the steadying influence of God's tender care.

When Ted and I first came to you in Riverside that night, we were edging ever closer to the precipice of divorce. You offered hope through Jesus, and little by little we began rebuilding our love, with small gestures at first. No more knife-licking, a handful of flowers picked by Ted with love, an ounce of understanding, and a pound of patience. And, Joyce, dear Joyce, with thanks to you and praise to Jesus—our love grew to the point that we can now stand together in the face of tremendous adversity and *know* that we're happier than we've ever been.

We have no money today, but we have peace, love, and a beautiful trust in our Saviour and Lord. He has never failed to provide for us and He is showing us daily just how very much He cares.

We couldn't have survived this year, Joyce, if you hadn't started us on the path of caring."

This beautiful couple began to make patient allowances for each other. The husband was willing to let Christ change Him, and the wife became eager to be all that God wanted her to be. Both of them have saved their marriage.

Accepting each other is my second emphasis. It's a tough assignment, but it's done by starting with the word *forgiveness*.

Again, let me write out Paul's words from Ephesians 4:32 (RSV). He said we are to "1. Be kind to one another, 2. tenderhearted, 3. forgiving one another, (Why?) as God in Christ forgave you."

If you have asked Christ to forgive you of your sins, remember—right now—how quickly that was accomplished even though God knows *all* about you.

His forgiveness was faster than TV's instant replay. Why is it we hesitate so long in forgiving our spouse, children, relatives, or neighbors?

If our homes are to experience the healing of broken hearts and spirits, we must return to God's remarkable ways.

The Bible cannot be the best seller which we take to church once a week. We must begin by living, acting, and breathing its time-honored principles.

Is it too tough a job? On the surface, yes. It is too hard to do on our own. But a great passage in Proverbs 3:4-6 says, "If you want favor with both God and man, and a reputation for good judgment and common sense, then trust the Lord completely; don't ever trust yourself. In everything you do, put God first, and He will direct you and crown your efforts with success" (TLB).

So success for the troubled Christian family is here for the reaching, the changing, and for the taking, but it will require both husband and wife to join hearts and hands and say with one voice, "As for me and my family—we will serve the Lord!"

From the Heart of Joyce Landorf

Joyce presents sparkling highlights from her best-selling books. The following four cassettes are also available as singles, for $4.98 each.

The Fragrance of Beauty ■ Skillfully shows how to achieve an inner beauty that outglows all others. *1LAN801*

His Stubborn Love ■ Joyce shares the reality of a marriage on the rocks as well as the answers she and her fusband found with God's help. These same answers may well improve your marriage, or a friend's! *1LAN802*

Mourning Song ■ With great sensitivity, Joyce talks about the tremendous trial of accepting one's own approaching death or that of a close family member. A truly inspirational and strengthening message. *1LAN803*

The Richest Lady in Town ■ Most women are passing up the wealth available through Christ as they seek artificial solutions to problems of personal fulfillment. *1LAN804*

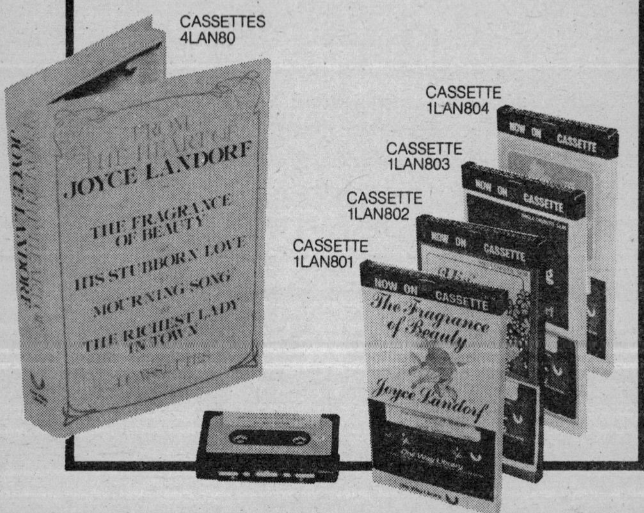

For These Fragile Times ■ At a time when human relationships are so easily shattered comes this cheerful message. Let Joyce tell you how life with those around you can become exciting and new! A refreshing breakthrough for developing lasting relationships. *Single Cassette $4.98 1LAN581*

Dinner Hour: Disaster or Delight ■ Don't let family feuds spoil another carefully planned and lovingly prepared dinner! Joyce offers hints for making mealtimes pleasant, sharing experiences for all family members. Bring your family together at the table tonight! *Single Cassette $4.98 1LAN02*

Tough and Tender ■ Joyce directs this message to men—as only a very sensitive and sensible wife and mother can. She's down to earth about the responsibilities of spiritual leadership in the home, and about "tuning in" to the daily considerations that can strengthen every marriage relationship. Every woman wants and can have a man that's tough and tender. *Single Cassette $4.98 1LAN01*

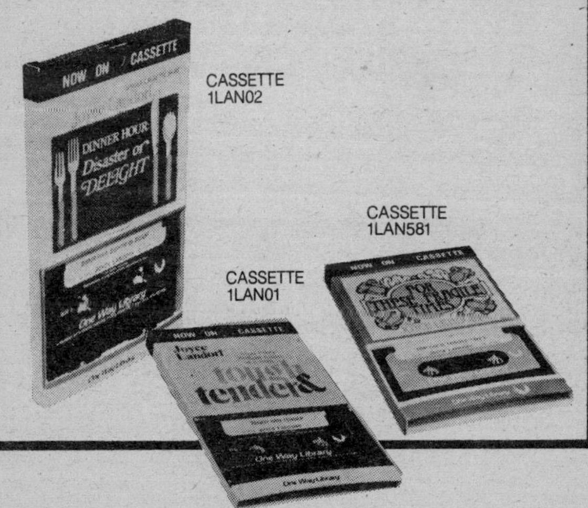